36 More Solos for Young Singers

Compiled by Joan Frey Boytim

To access companion recorded accompaniments online, visit:
www.halleonard.com/mylibrary

Enter Code
7276-4884-0774-0311

ISBN 978-1-4584-1781-7

HAL•LEONARD®

Visit Hal Leonard Online at
www.halleonard.com

Contact us:
Hal Leonard
7777 West Bluemound Road
Milwaukee, WI 53213
Email: info@halleonard.com

In Europe, contact:
Hal Leonard Europe Limited
42 Wigmore Street
Marylebone, London, W1U 2RN
Email: info@halleonardeurope.com

In Australia, contact:
Hal Leonard Australia Pty. Ltd.
4 Lentara Court
Cheltenham, Victoria, 3192 Australia
Email: info@halleonard.com.au

CONTENTS

The price of this publication includes access to companion recorded accompaniments online, for download or streaming, using the unique code found on the title page. Visit **www.halleonard.com/mylibrary** and enter the access code.

Pianist on the recordings: Laura Ward

PREFACE

A current trend in many private studios and community music schools is to offer voice lessons to students who, just decades ago, would be considered too young for serious one-on-one vocal instruction. As more upper elementary, junior high or middle school students seek such opportunities for study, it is a challenge for teachers to find solo books with appropriate repertoire to meet the needs of these students. With those boys and girls in mind, *36 Solos for Young Singers* was compiled. Offered with a convenient companion compact disc of piano accompaniments, recorded by a professional pianist, this collection serves as a beginning studio volume, as a collection for motivated students to explore solo singing on their own, or with the help of a voice teacher, school music teacher, choir director, or simply for family fun singing sessions.

The popularity of producing musical shows in late elementary and middle schools and community theater groups for children has also led to a great increase of students studying private voice. *36 Solos for Young Singers* has proved to be a widely used book for many of these students. Teachers expressed a need for another comparable volume for this same age group.

The format and type of songs in *36 More Solos for Young Singers* is very similar. Most songs can be sung by anyone. A few such as "Ragtime Cowboy Joe," "For Me and My Gal," and "My Friend John" will be enjoyed by boys, while "Charlie Is My Darling," "Gently, Johnny, My Jingalo," and "My Soldier" are specifically included for girls.

The ranges have been kept primarily from D to D with some exceptions. These melodic songs include humorous, folk, spirituals, sentimental, and nostalgic selections. A number of the songs may be unfamiliar to some, yet are worthy of inclusion. The many styles of music introduce the singer to varied musical challenges within the framework of this beginning type of repertoire.

May you enjoy having more songs to introduce to this age level as well as to older beginning students who enjoy singing for pure pleasure.

Joan Frey Boytim

Alpine Song

James Vila Blake
(From the German)

John Ireland

shep - herd lad, Thou hap - py boy, like thee, Thou hap - py boy, like

thee! 2. Then would I sing till

ech - oes wild From rock to val - ley rang, Till to my voice, in

all the world, Each heart re-joic-ing sprang. ___ The Al - pine rose its

sweet-ness sheds, ___ Down from the hills a - long; O

moun-tain love, so fresh and free, Bear swift-ly on my song, Bear

swift-ly on my song!

8vb

The Band Played On

John F. Palmer

Charles B. Ward

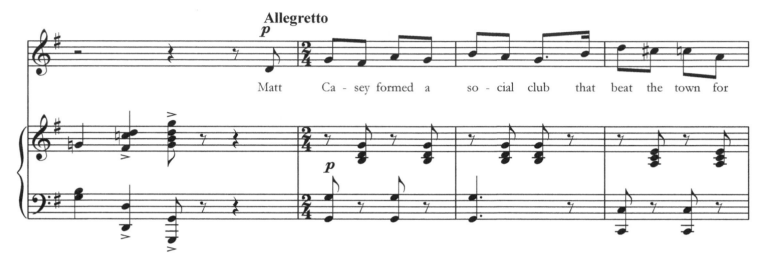

wax. And danced with noise and vig - or at the ball, _____

_____ Each Sat - ur - day you'd see them dressed up in Sun - day

clothes, Each lad would have his sweet - heart by his side. _____ When

Ca - sey led the first grand march they all would fall in line, Be -

hind the man who was their joy and pride, _____ For _____

Valse

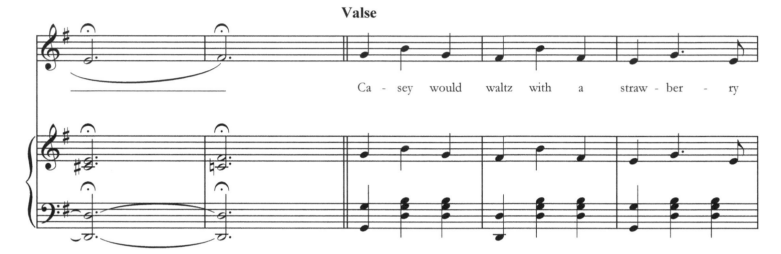

_____ Ca - sey would waltz with a straw - ber - ry

blonde, And the Band played on, _____ He'd

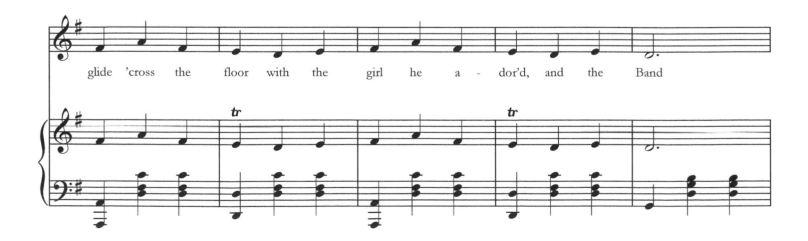

glide 'cross the floor with the girl he a - dor'd, and the Band

Buffalo Gals
(Won't You Come Out Tonight?)

Words and Music by
Cool White (John Hodges)
First published 1844

Buf - fa - lo gals, won't ya come out to - night, won't ya
Yes, pret - ty boys, we'll come out to - night, we'll

come out to - night, won't ya come out to - night? Buf - fa - lo gals, won't ya
come out to - night, we'll come out to - night. Yes, pret - ty boys, we'll

come out to - night and dance by the light of the moon?
come out to - night and dance by the light of the moon.

I

danced with a gal with a hole in her stock - ing and her heel kept a - rock - in' and her

toe kept a - knock - in'. I danced with a gal with a hole in her stock - ing, and we

danced by the light of the moon.

1

moon.

2

sfz

Bury Me Not on the Lone Prairie

Rev. Edwin H. Chapin

Cowboy Ballad, 1870s
Attributed to H. Clemens of South Dakota
Music by Ossian N. Dodge

A parody based on the 1849 song "The Ocean Burial"

Cradle Song

English translation by Edward Oxenford

Wilhelm Taubert

Andantino con moto

Sleep, my lit - tle one; See, the sun has gone;

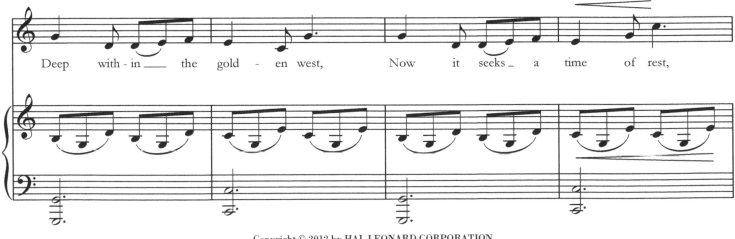

Deep with - in the gold - en west, Now it seeks a time of rest,

Shades of night a - round are fall - ing, Shep - herds to their flocks are call - ing;

La - bor for the day is done; Sleep, my lit - tle one.

Sleep, my dar - ling, sleep; Watch o'er thee __ I keep;

In the vale __ the night - in - gale Trills its sil - - ver - not - - ed tale.

All the flow - ers now are clos - ing, Pet - als fair to rest com - pos - ing,

Till the rays of morn - ing peep, Sleep, my dar - ling, sleep!

For Me and My Gal

Edgar Leslie and E. Ray Goetz

George W. Meyer

Ev - 'ry - bod - y's been know - ing_____ To a wed - ding they're go - ing_____ And for weeks they've been sew - ing,_____

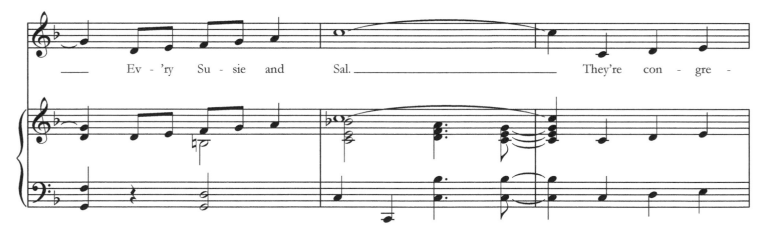

_____ Ev - 'ry Su - sie and Sal._____ They're con - gre -

gat - ing_____ for me and my gal,_____ The Par - son's

wait - ing _____ for me and my gal. _____ And some - time

I'm goin' to build a lit - tle home for two, __ For three or four __ or

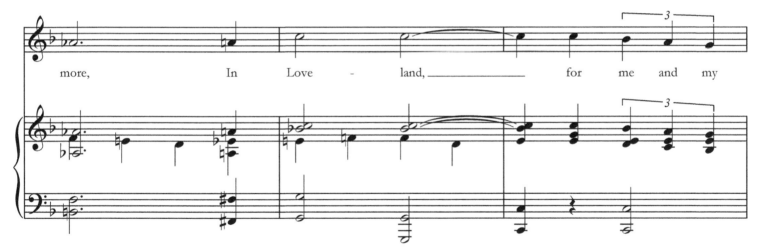

more, In Love - land, _____ for me and my

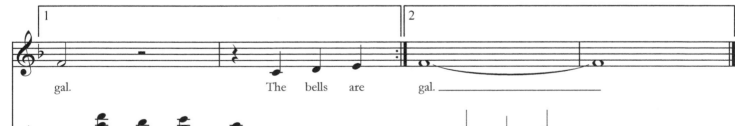

gal. The bells are gal. _____ gal.

Four-Leaf Clover

Ella Higginson

Leila M. Brownell

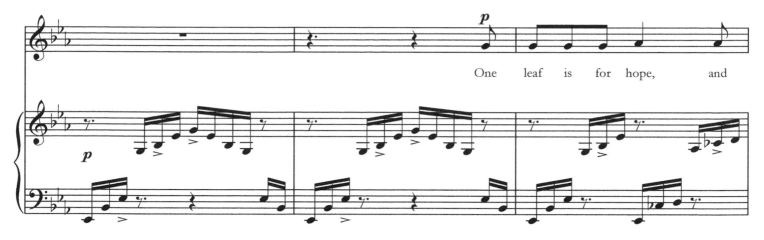

One leaf is for hope, and

one is for faith, And one is for love, you know, And

God put an - oth - er one in for luck. If you search, you will find where they

grow. But

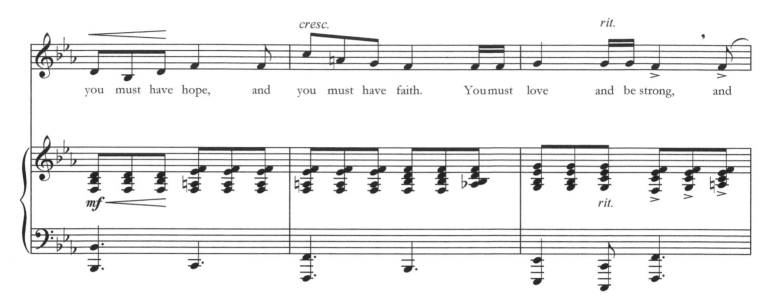

you must have hope, and you must have faith. You must love and be strong, and

so, _____ If you work, if you wait, you will find the place where the

four - leaf clo - vers grow.

To my Sister Lizzie

Grandfather's Clock

Words and Music by
Henry Clay Work

bought on the morn of that day that he was born, And was al - ways his treas - ure and
struck twen - ty - four when he en - tered at the door, With a bloom - ing and beau - ti - ful

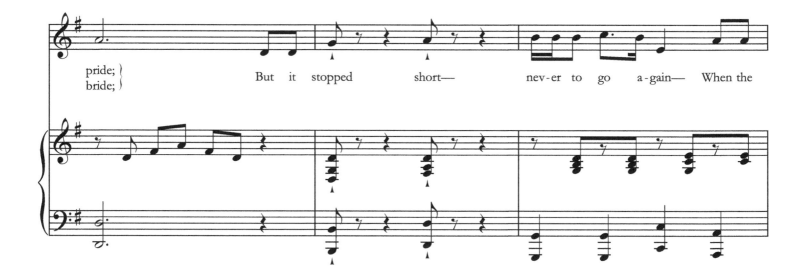

pride; }
bride; }
But it stopped short— nev - er to go a - gain— When the

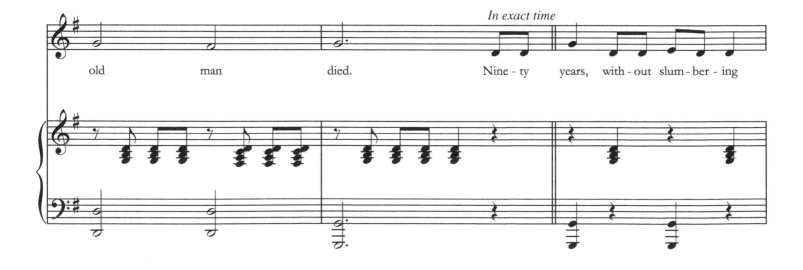

old man died. Nine - ty years, with - out slum - ber - ing

In exact time

(tick, tick, tick, tick), His life - sec - onds num - ber - ing (tick, tick, tick, tick), It

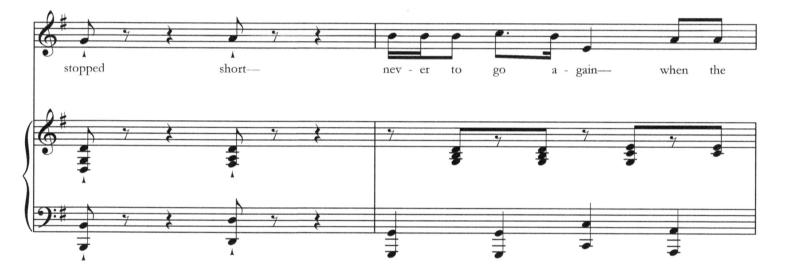

stopped   short—   nev - er to go a - gain—   when the

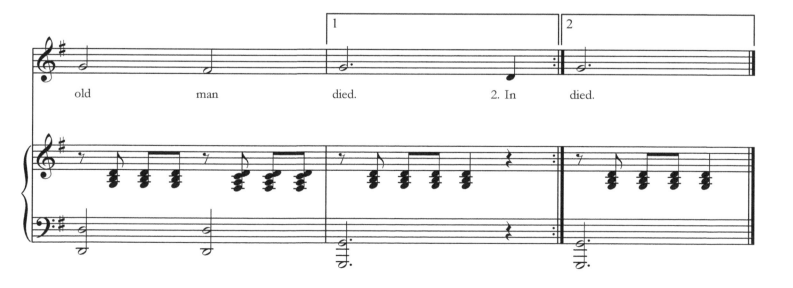

old   man   died.   2. In   died.

Gently, Johnny, My Jingalo

Collected and arranged by
Cecil J. Sharp

The Glendy Burk

Words and Music by
Stephen C. Foster

Moderately fast

The Glen-dy Burk is a might-y fast boat, with a might-y fast cap-tain too; He sits up there on the hur-ri-cane roof And he keeps his eyes on the crew. I can't stay here, for they work too hard; I'm bound to leave this

la-dy love is as pret-ty as a pink,_ I'll meet_ her on the way I'll take her back to the sun-ny old south_ And there I'll make her_ stay So don't you fret my_ hon-ey dear, Oh! don't you fret Miss

town; I'll take my duds and tote 'em on my back When the Glen - dy Burk comes
Brown I'll take you back 'fore the mid - dle of the week When the Glen - dy Burk comes

down.
down.

Ho! for Lou' - si - an - a! I'm bound to leave this town; I'll

take my duds and tote 'em on my back When the Glen - dy Burk comes down. My

1

2

down.

His Favorite Flower

William W. Lowitz

Tempo di Gavotte

She was a dain - ty lit - tle miss And he was ver - y

tall, And they gath - ered all the flow - ers That grew by the gar - den

wall. "My fa - vor - ite is the rose" she said, "Don't

you pre - fer the pink? Per - haps you like the hol - ly - hock, You're

Somewhat slower

opt. just like them, I think. But tell me now your fa - vor - ite flower, For

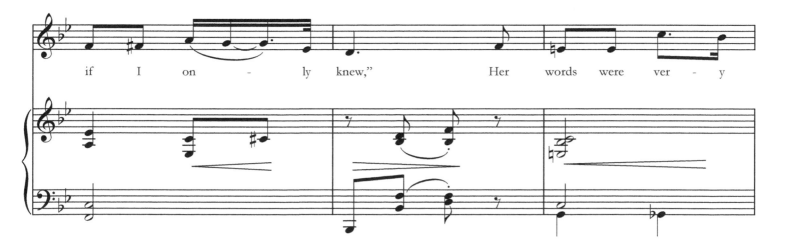

if I on - ly knew," Her words were ver - y

low and sweet, "I'd try and raise a few."   "My   fa - vor - ite

flow - er,   This   mo - ment   I   can   see, _____   I'm

con passione

look - ing   at   your   tu - lips,   Will you raise tu - lips for me? _____   I'm

look - ing   at   your   tu - lips,   Will you raise tu - lips for me?

Hey! Pretty Lady
A Ballad

Words and Music by
Louis James Boulter

1. Joy - ful - ly, joy - ful - ly, how the bells ring,
2. A - men is said, and these two are made one,

Peal - ing a mes - sage that makes the heart sing; They tell me that some - one will
Names must be reg - is - tered ere all is done; The folk are all wait - ing im -

mar - ry to - day The pret - ti - est maid - en that lives round this way. And
pa - tient - ly there, To feast their eyes well on this hap - py young pair. O,

ev - 'ry - one's hap - py this bright day of June, With birds all a - sing - ing, and
there they are, look! Did you e'er see such charm? A dain - ty hand grace - ful - ly

bells all a - tune; They're off to the wed - ding so blithe and so gay, And
slipped through his arm! Nay, all will a - gree, she's the love - li - est bride That

here's what the bells are all try - ing to say: Hey! pret - ty la - dy, we're
ev - er a - way from the old church did ride. Hey! pret - ty la - dy, we're

ring - ing for you, Ring - ing for you and a bride - groom true;
ring - ing for you, Wish - ing you hap - pi - ness all your life through,

Man - y's the time that we've rung out be - fore, But you are so charm - ing we'll
Charm - ing you look, and so charm - ing you are, That's why we are ring - ing our

ring it _____ the more. _____
mes - sage _____ a -

far. _____

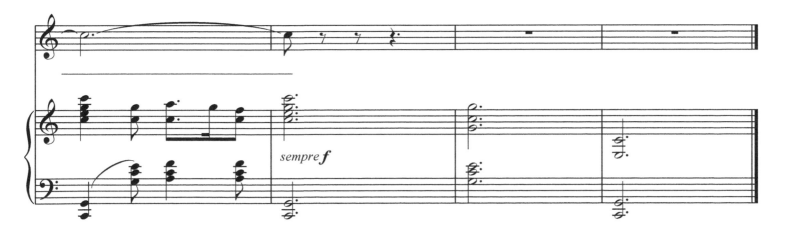

I Heard You Go By

Kathleen Stuart

Daniel Wood

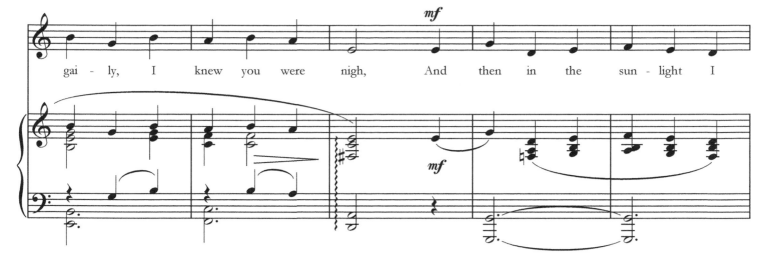

gai - ly, I knew you were nigh, And then in the sun - light I

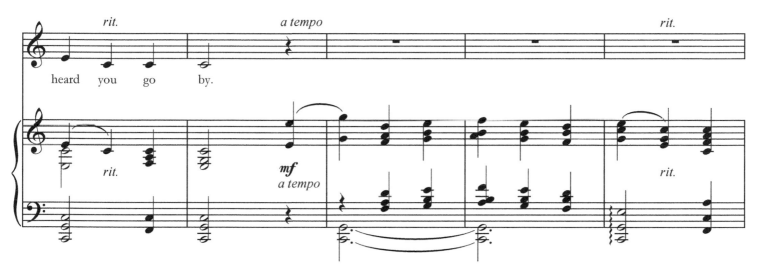

heard you go by.

Oh, dark was the mid - night, A star peep - ing through, As

I lay a - dream - ing, A - dream - ing of you. So

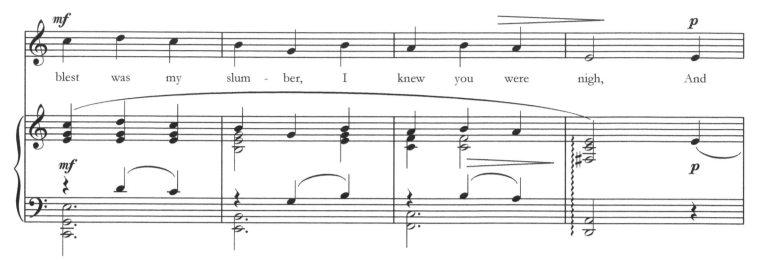

blest was my slum - ber, I knew you were nigh, And

then in the star - light I heard you go by. So

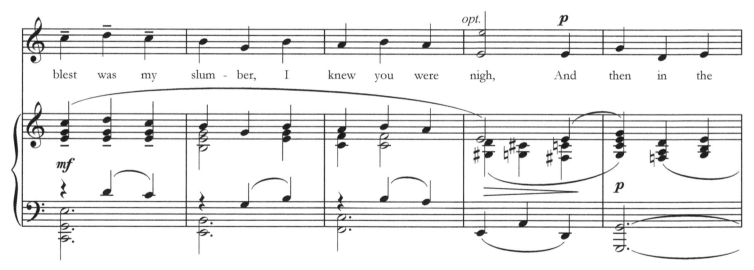

blest was my slum - ber, I knew you were nigh, And then in the

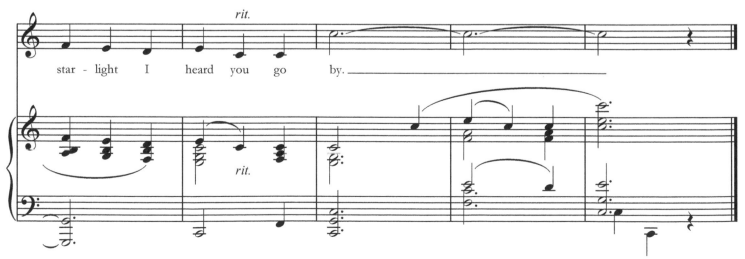

star - light I heard you go by.

I'm Forever Blowing Bubbles

Jaan Kenbrovin*

John William Kellette

*Collective pseudonym for James Kendis, James Brockman, and Nat Vincent.

They're born a - new their days are few

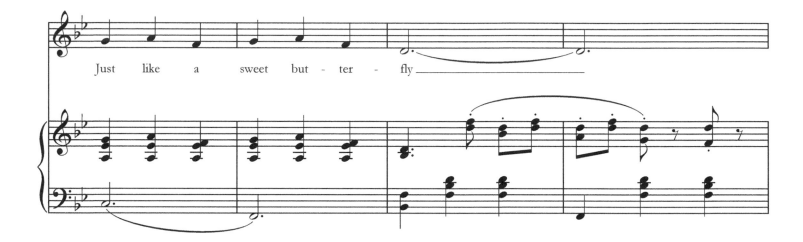

Just like a sweet but - ter - fly _____

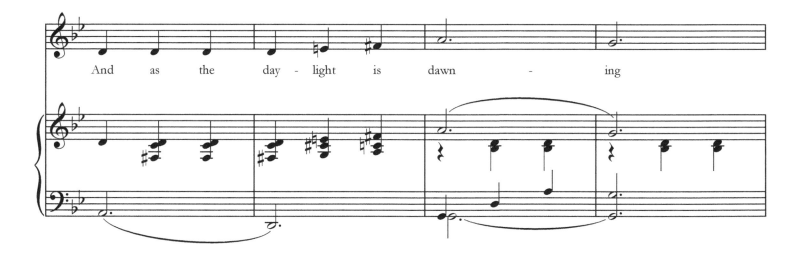

And as the day - light is dawn - ing

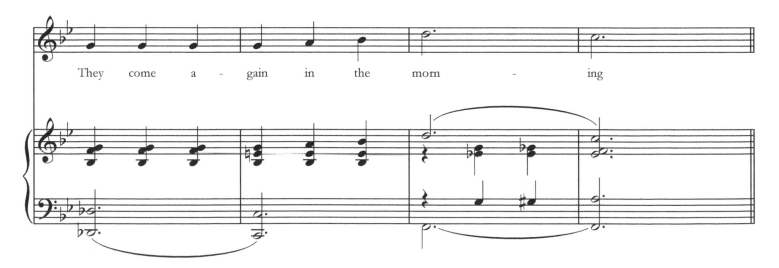

They come a - gain in the morn - ing

I'm _____ for - ev - er blow - ing bub - bles _____

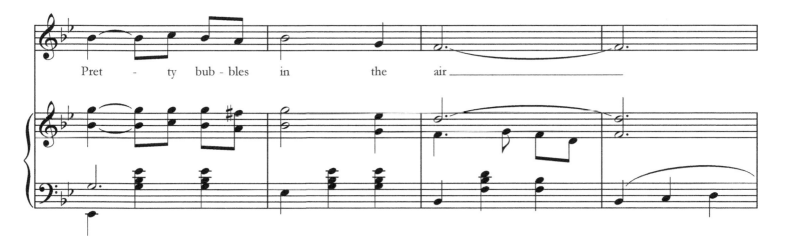

Pret - ty bub - bles in the air _____

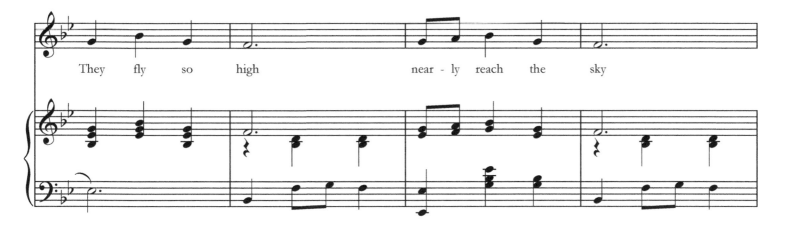

They fly so high near - ly reach the sky

Then like my dreams they fade and die

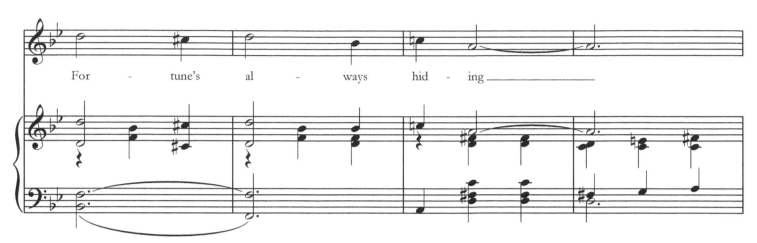

For - tune's al - ways hid - ing _____

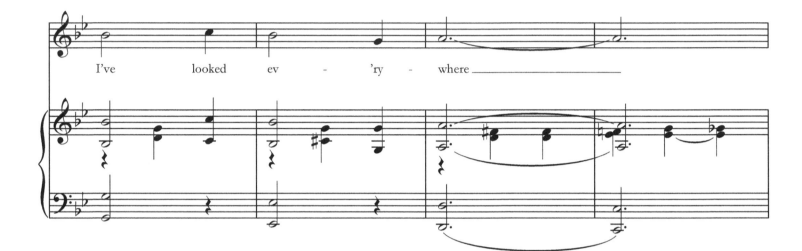

I've looked ev - 'ry - where _____

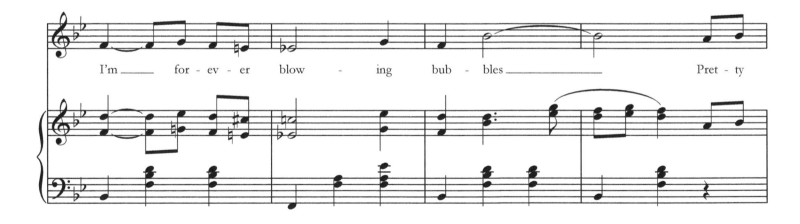

I'm _____ for - ev - er blow - ing bub - bles _____ Pret - ty

bub - bles in the air. _____

Ja-Da
(Ja Da, Ja Da, Jing Jing Jing!)

Words and Music by
Bob Carleton

going to win you thru and thru.____ There ain't much to the words but the

mu - sic is grand, _ And you'll be sing-ing it to beat _ the band. _ Now

you've heard of your _ "Will O' the Wisp," But give a lit-tle lis-ten to

With lots of Ja Da

this: _____ It goes Ja* Da, ____ Ja Da, ____ Ja Da, Ja Da, Jing,** Jing,

f   (Ja Da,)   (Ja Da,)

*Pronounced "Yah"
**Pronounced "Jing" as in "Jingle"

Listen to the Mocking Bird

Alice Hawthorne

Richard Milburn

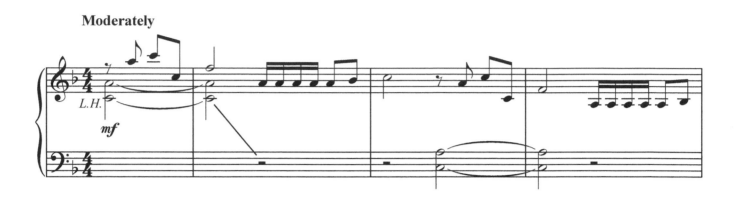

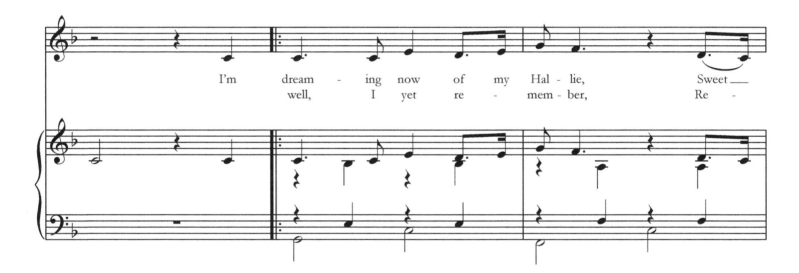

mock - ing bird, Lis - ten to the mock - ing bird, The

mock - ing bird still sing - ing o'er her grave, Lis - ten to the

mock - ing bird, Lis - ten to the mock - ing bird Still

sing - ing where the weep - ing wil - lows wave. Ah, wave.

Memories

Gus Kahn

Egbert Van Alstyne

52

veal - ing _____ mem - 'ries of love's gold - en dawn. _____

Slowly

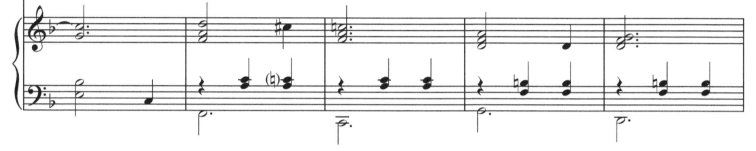

____ Mem - o - ries, mem - o - ries,

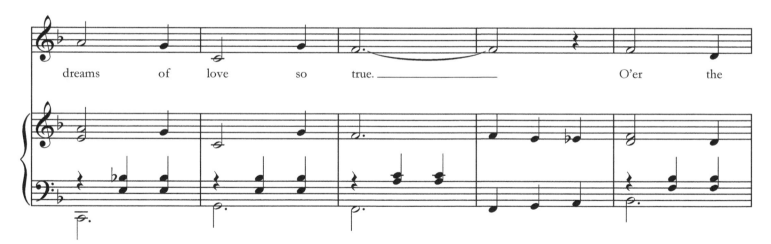

dreams of love so true. _____ O'er the

Sea of Mem - o - ry I'm drift - ing back to

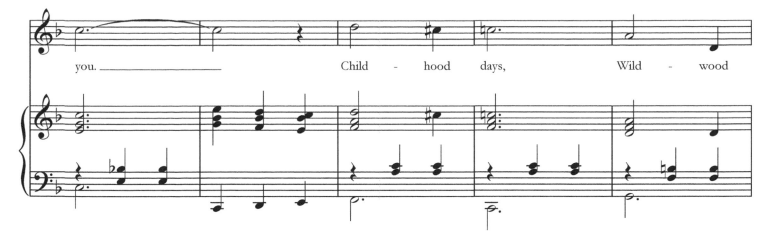

you. _____ Child - hood days, Wild - wood

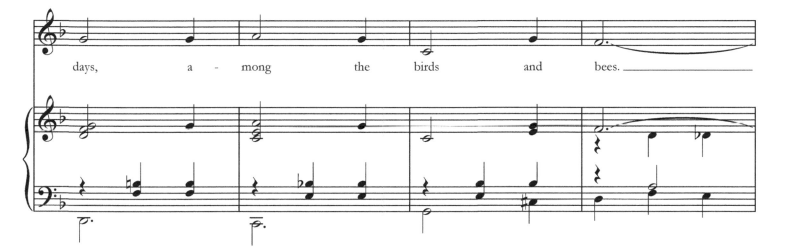

days, a - mong the birds and bees. _____

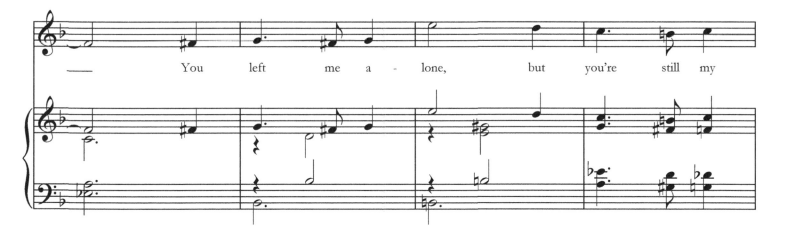

_____ You left me a - lone, but you're still my

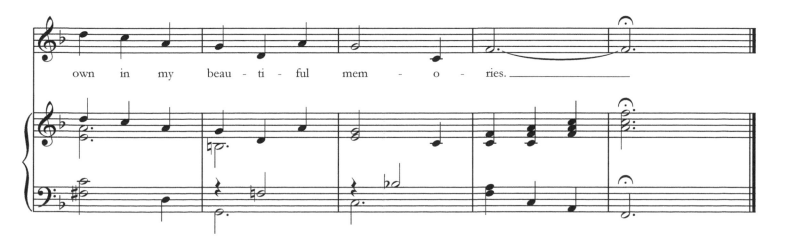

own in my beau - ti - ful mem - o - ries. _____

Love's Wondrous Garden

Annie Andros Hawley

Walter Lewis

When first I came in-to my gar - den 'twas lone - ly, Song - birds were si - lent, o - ver - cast, the skies; The gates swung wide, you came, a won-drous vi - sion, My gar - den fair was changed to Par - a - dise.

My Old Friend John

John Legge

Edward Land
arr. Charles Fonteyn Manney

In moderate time

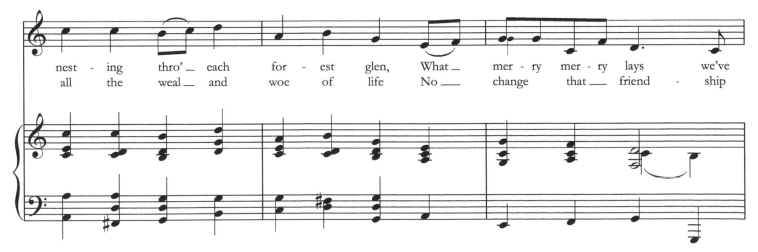

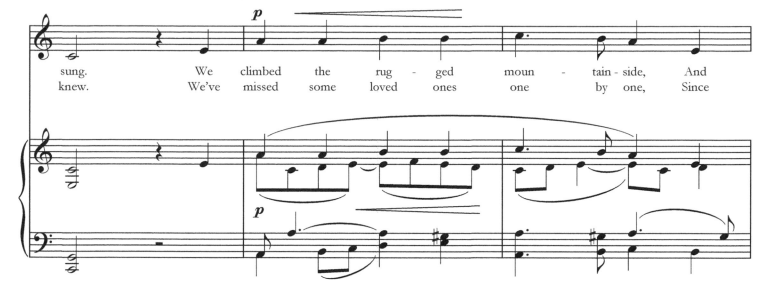

sung.   We   climbed   the   rug - ged   moun - tain - side,   And

knew.   We've   missed   some   loved   ones   one   by   one,   Since

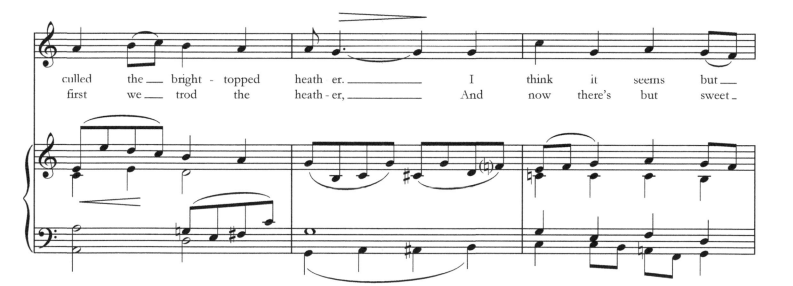

culled   the   bright - topped   heath er.   I   think   it   seems   but

first   we   trod   the   heath - er,   And   now   there's   but   sweet

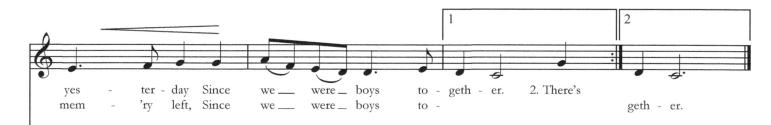

yes - ter - day   Since   we   were   boys   to - geth - er.   2. There's

mem - 'ry left,   Since   we   were   boys   to -   geth - er.

My Soldier

English translation by Edward Thatcher

German Folksong (1828)

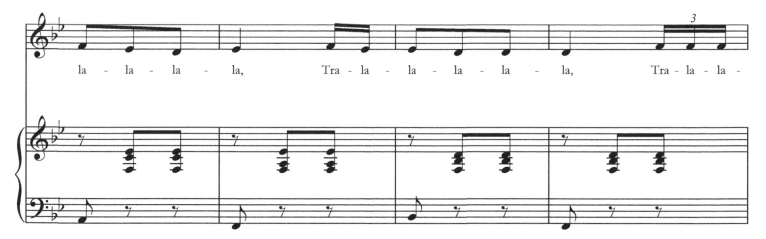

la - la - la - la, Tra - la - la - la - la - la, Tra - la - la -

la - la, tra - la - la la - la, tra - la - la - la - la, Tra - la - la -

la - la, tra - la - la la - la, tra - la - la - la - la.

The Night Wind
(The Sunbeam and the Rose)

J. Keirn Brennan

Ernest R. Ball

soul full of sun - shine knows.

But o - ver the sun - beam sleep — ing, The

night wind came — in play, — And the sun - beam at dawn, Found the

rose - bud torn, And the night wind flown a - way. —

O No, John!

Collected and arranged by
Cecil J. Sharp

Allegro moderato

1. On

yon - der hill there stands a ___ crea - ture; Who she is I do not know.
Mad - am, I will give you ___ jew - els; I will make you rich and free;

I'll go and court her for her ___ beau - ty; She must an - swer Yes or No.
I will ___ give you silk - en ___ dress - es. Mad - am will you mar - ry me?

Oh, Charlie Is My Darling

Variously attributed to
James Hogg or Lady Carolina Nairne

Traditional Scottish Song
Accompaniment by Helen Hopekirk

*Claymore: A Scottish sword used circa 1400–1700.

Char - lie came to our ___ town, The ___ young ___ Chev - a - lier. 2. As
as the folks came run - nin' out, To ___ meet the Chev - a - lier. 3. With
came to fight for Scot - land's right, And the

young ___ Chev - a - lier. Oh, Char - lie is my dar - ling, my

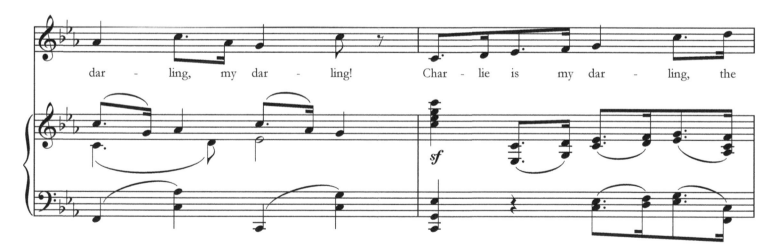

dar - ling, my dar - ling! Char - lie is my dar - ling, the

young Chev - a - lier. 4. They've

left their bon - nie High - land hills, Their wives and bairn - ies* dear, To
there were man - y beat - ing hearts, And man - y a hope and fear, And

draw the sword for Scot - land's lord, The _ brave _ Chev - a - lier. 5. Oh,
man - y were the pray'rs put up for the young _ Chev - a - lier. Oh,

Char - lie is my dar - ling, my dar - ling, my dar - ling! Char - lie is my dar - ling, the

young Chev - a - lier.

*Bairnies: A Scottish term of endearment for small children. Pronounced "bare knees."

Ragtime Cowboy Joe

Words and Music by Lewis F. Muir,
Grant Clarke and Maurice Abrahams

sings _____ swing - y mu - sic to the cat - tle as he

swings, _____ back and for - ward in the sad - dle on a

horse _____ that is syn - co - pat - ed gait - ed, and there's

such a fun - ny me - ter to the sound of his re - peat - er, how they

run _____ when they hear that fel - low's guns, be - cause the

West - ern folks all know, he's a high fa - lut - in', scoot - in', shoot - in',

son of a gun from Ar - i - zo - na, rag - time cow - boy, oh! what a cow - boy,

Rag - time Cow - boy Joe. He al - ways Joe.

The Old Woman and the Peddler

Anonymous

English Folksong

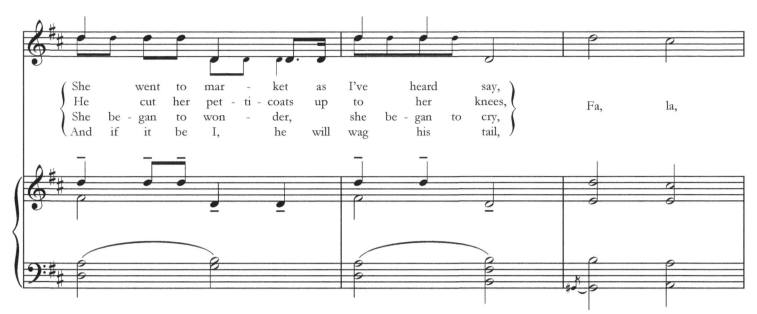

She went to mar - ket as I've heard say,
He cut her pet - ti - coats up to her knees,
She be - gan to won - der, she be - gan to cry,
And if it be I, he will wag his tail,

Fa, la,

la la la la la!

She __ fell a - sleep on the King's high - way,
Which made the old __ wom - an to shiv - er and sneeze,
"Oh, __ dear - y me, this can nev - er be I!"
And if it's not __ I, he will bark and wail."

mf

mf

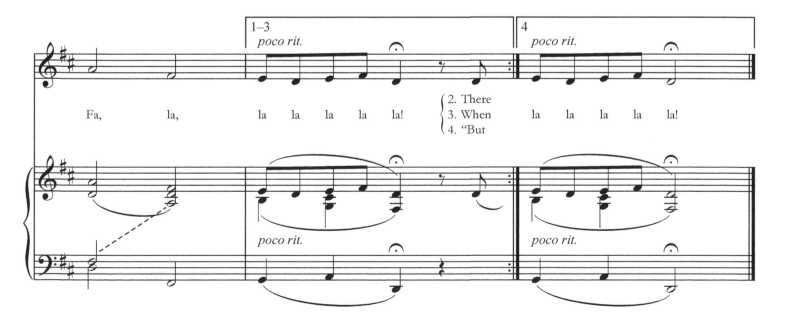

Fa, la, la la la la la!

2. There
3. When
4. "But

la la la la la!

poco rit.

poco rit.

poco rit.

poco rit.

Peace of Night

Georg Scherer
English translation by Elizabeth M. Traquair

Carl Reinecke

Moderate time

The sun has long de-part - ed, The

day to-night doth — yield; And peace, so still and ho - ly, Broods

o - ver house and — field. To wear - ied eye - lids gent - ly The

night brings sweet-est sleep, And in each lit-tle cham - ber God's an-gel watch doth

keep. He __ lulls with song so gen - tle The babe to sweet re -

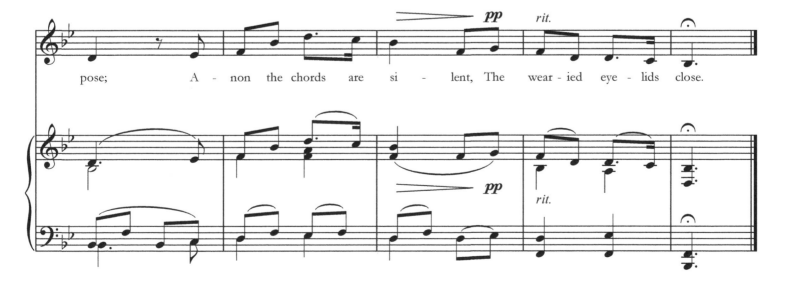

pose; A - non the chords are si - lent, The wear-ied eye - lids close.

Ring the Bluebell

Fred G. Bowles

Herbert Bunning

Rowing

P. Guglielmo

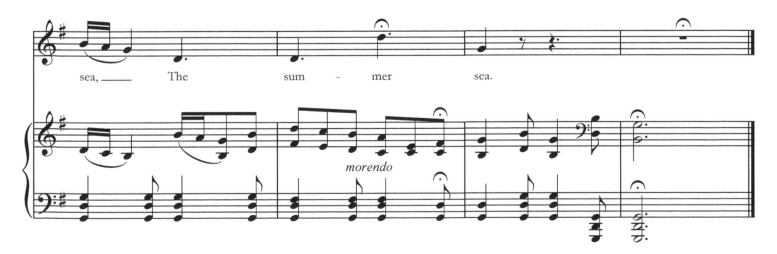

Shenandoah

American Folksong
about the Shenandoah Valley of Virginia

Various versions of this folksong exist, some about an Iroquois chief and his daughter; a later, 19th century sea chantey version was sometimes sung for weighing anchor.

Smilin' Through

Lyric and Music by
Arthur A. Penn

lit - tle green gate ___ At whose trel - lis I wait, ___ While two

eyes o' blue Come smil - in' through At me! ___ There's a

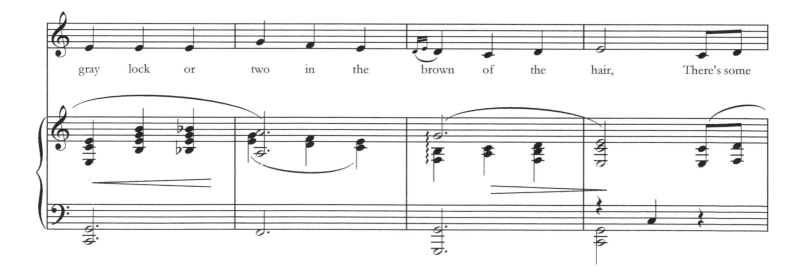

gray lock or two in the brown of the hair, There's some

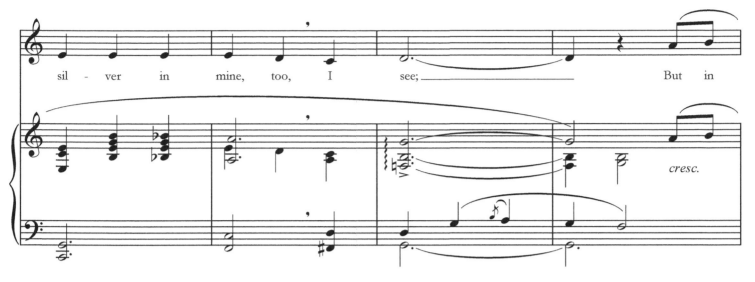

sil - ver in mine, too, I see; ____ But in

all the long years ___ When the clouds brought their tears, ___ Those two

eyes o' blue Kept smil - in' through At me! ____

Spring

J. Vila Blake
(from the German)

John Ireland

Allegro con grazia (♩ = 96-100)

1. Love - ly Spring, O___ come thou hith - er, Spring be - lov'd, O come a -
2. To the moun - tain__ I would wan - der, Rev - el in the val - leys__

gain;___ Bring us blos - soms, leaves and sing - ing,
green,___ On the sweet grass and the blos - soms

Deck a - gain the field and plain, Deck a - gain

Lie, and drink the sun - lit scene, Lie, and drink

the field and plain.

the sun - lit scene.

lusingando

Ped. ✱

1

2

3. I would hear the shep - herd pip - ing, I would hear the sheep - bell

ring, _____ And re - joic - ing on the mead - ow,

I would hear the __ bird - ies sing, _____ I would hear _____

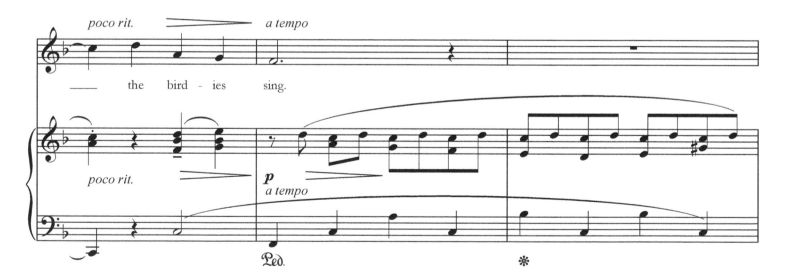

poco rit. *a tempo*

____ the bird - ies sing.

There stands a little man

from the opera *Hansel and Gretel*

Adelheid Wette
English translation by Constance Bache

Engelbert Humperdinck

* "Mankin," from the original German "Männlein," literally translates to mean "little man."

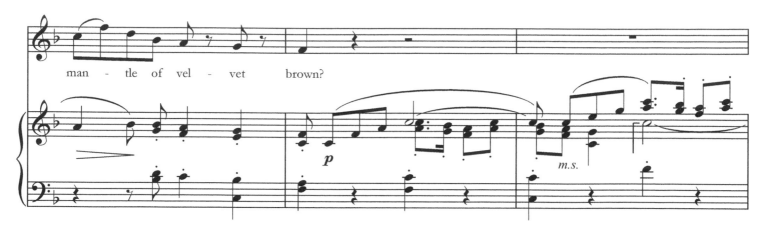

man - tle of vel - vet brown?

His hair is all of gold and his cheeks are

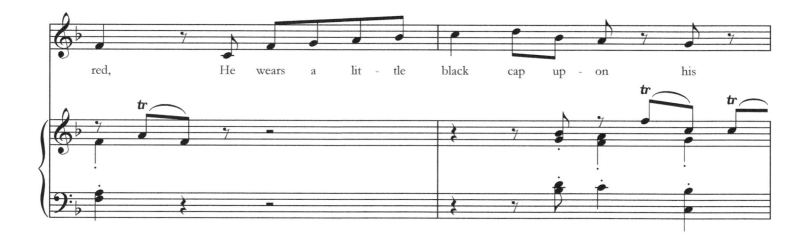

red, He wears a lit - tle black cap up - on his

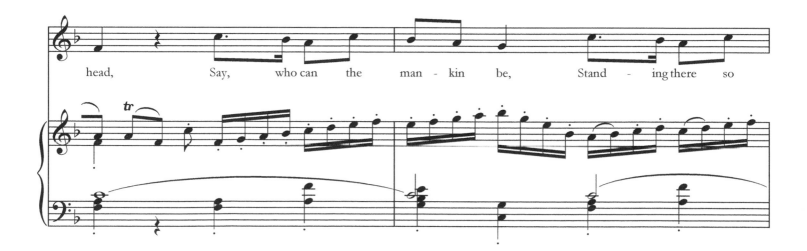

head, Say, who can the man - kin be, Stand - ing there so

si - lent - ly, With the lit - tle black __ cap up - on his

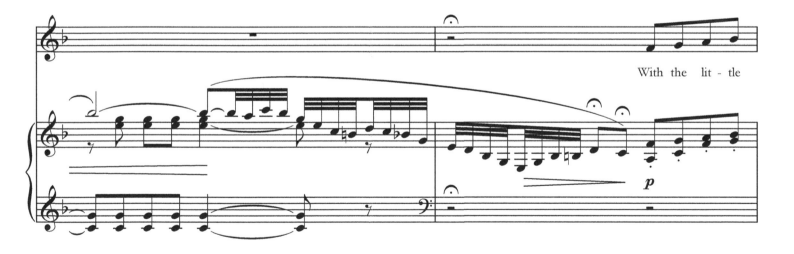

head?

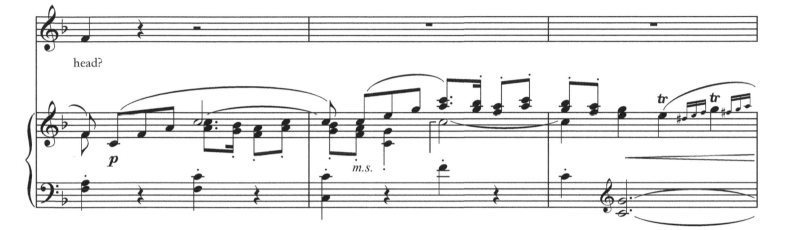

With the lit - tle

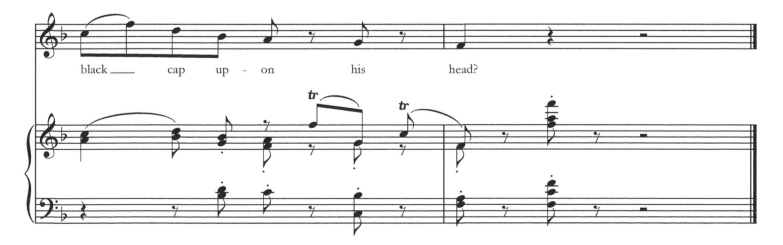

black __ cap up - on his head?

This Little Light of Mine

African-American Spiritual

I'm gon-na let it shine ____ ev-'ry day, ev-'ry

To Coda ⊕

day, ev-'ry day, ev-'ry day ____ gon-na let my lit-tle light

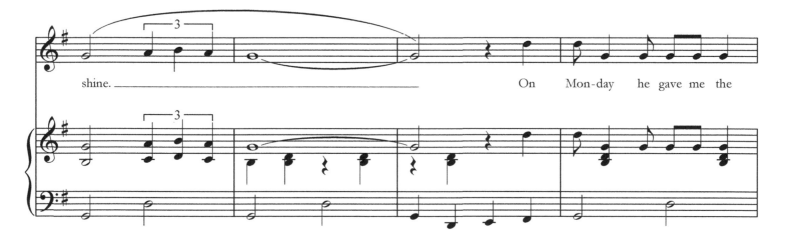

shine. _____ On Mon-day he gave me the

gift of love, on Tues-day peace came from a-bove, on Wednes-day told me to

have more faith, on Thurs - day gave me a lit - tle more grace. On

Fri - day told me to watch and pray, on Sat - ur - day told me just

what to say, on Sun - day gave me the pow - er di - vine, just to

D.S. al Coda

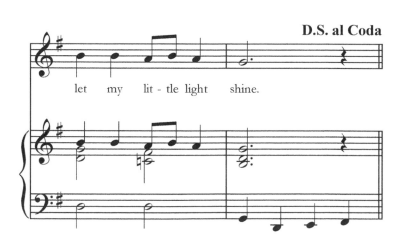

let my lit - tle light shine.

CODA

shine. _____

Wait for the Wagon

American Folksong
Arranged by George P. Knauff

Moderately

mf

1. Will you

come with me my Phil - lis, dear, to yon blue moun - tain free, Where the
2. you be - lieve my Phil - lis, dear, old Mike with all his wealth, Can

blos - soms smell the sweet - est, come rove a - long with me. It's
make you half so hap - py, as I with youth and health? We'll

ev - 'ry Sun - day morn - ing when I am by your side, We'll
have a lit - tle farm, a horse, a pig and cow; And

jump in - to the wag - on, and all take a ride.
you will mind the dair - y, while I will guide the plough.

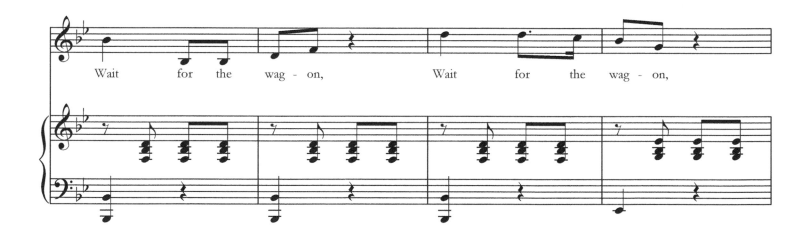

Wait for the wag - on, Wait for the wag - on,

Wait for the wag - on and we'll all take a ride.

Wait for the wag - on, wait for the wag - on,

wait for the wag - on and we'll all take a ride. 2. Do

ride.

The Train for Poppyland

Edgar Wade Abbot

Grenville D. Wilson

pal - ace car is the moth - er's arms; The whis-tle a low, sweet strain; The

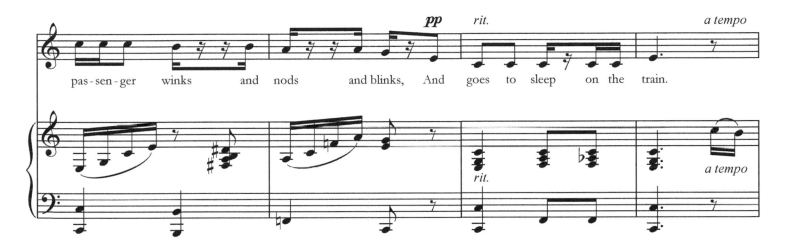

pas - sen - ger winks and nods and blinks, And goes to sleep on the train.

At 8 P. M. the

next train starts For the pop - py land a - far, The sum - mons clear falls

on the ear, "All a - board for the sleep - ing car!" But what is the fare to ___

pop - py land? I hope it is not too dear; The fare is this— a

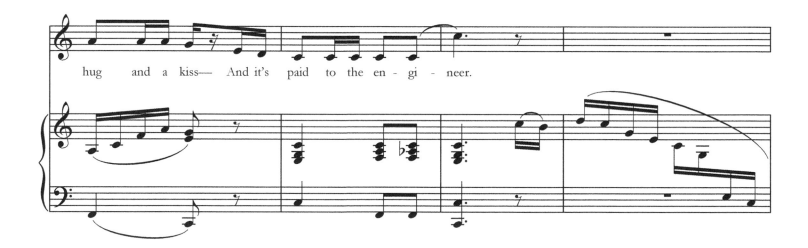

hug and a kiss— And it's paid to the en - gi - neer.

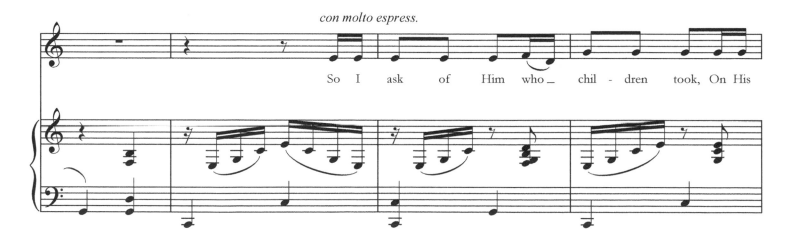

con molto espress.

So I ask of Him who ___ chil - dren took, On His

knees in kind - ness great, "Take charge, I pray, of the trains each day, That

leave at 6 and 8. Keep watch on the pas - sen - gers," thus I pray, "For to

me they are ver - y dear; And spe - cial ward, O gra - cious Lord, O'er the

gen - tle en - gi - neer."

The World Is Waiting for the Sunrise

Eugene Lockhart

Ernest Seitz

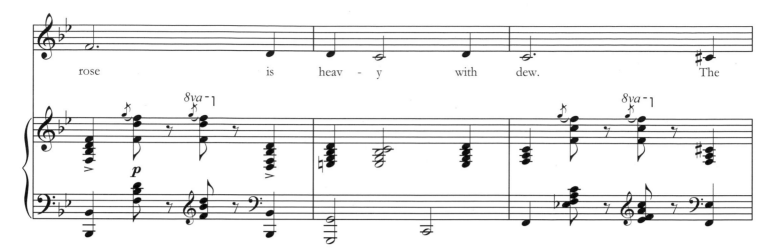

rose is heav - y with dew. The

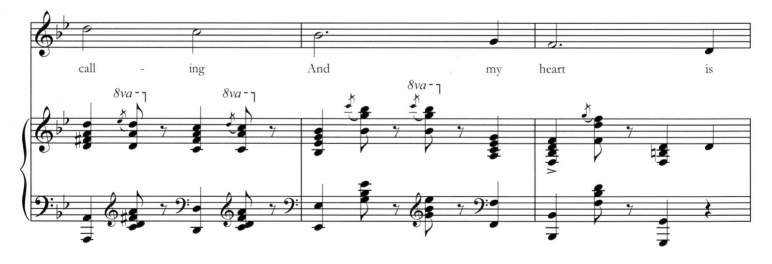

thrush on high, his sleep - y mate is

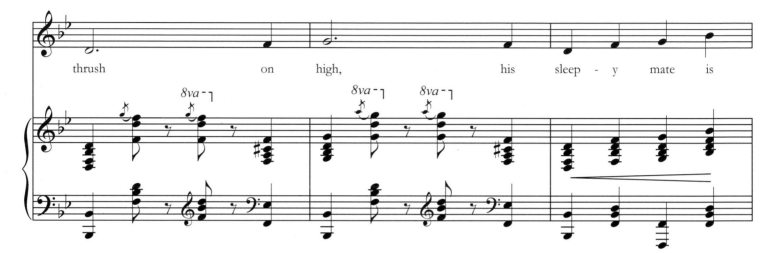

call - ing And my heart is

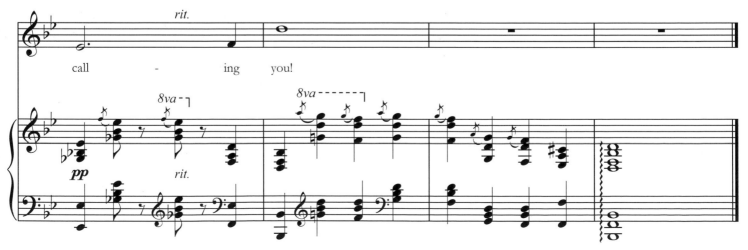

call - ing you!